THE BIBLE READ-TO-ME

ABC
BOOK

For Big and Little People to Enjoy Together

A NOTE TO GROWN-UPS

This is not just a SIT-AND-LISTEN book. It is a THINK-AND-LEARN book—a TALK-IT-OVER book. Sometimes kids grow up thinking that books about the Bible are old-fashioned and boring. Although each letter of the alphabet focuses upon one or more specific Bible story, event, or idea, this book was made for FUN. Both text and illustrations were created to spark the child's imagination, appeal to his sense of wonder, and kindle his interest in the truth of God's Word.

Reading aloud to a child may be the single most significant contribution a parent or grown-up friend can make to a child's academic success, for reading *to* children is the best way to develop their ability to read *for* and *by* themselves.

Very young children are intrigued by the sound of language and will enjoy hearing the rhythmic alliteration found in the key phrases of this book. Beginning readers whose reading vocabulary may be only a few hundred words, but who enjoy a listening vocabulary of well over 10,000 words, will profit from the expressive oral reading of language that is a step beyond their own reading level. And they will respond to the challenge of expanding their limited sight vocabulary.

These statements, though true, may, however, *not* be the best reasons for a grown-up to share this book with a child. Children cherish uninterrupted time alone with a "comfortable" adult. The affection and togetherness enjoyed by both grown-up and child in these quiet, cloistered moments make for memories that reach far beyond the pages of a book.

ABC's are basic "handles" in a child's educational development. Quality time spent with parents and adult friends is important to his psychological and emotional well-being. The message of God's Word is basic to every other area of his life. In the shared use of this book lies a delightful opportunity to meet the real needs of young lives . . . lovingly. Seize and enjoy!

Joy MacKenzie

THE BIBLE READ-TO-ME

ABC
BOOK

For Big and Little People to Enjoy Together

Joy MacKenzie
Illustrated by Kathleen Bullock

Chariot Books
David C. Cook Publishing Co.

To nieces Sara and Jessie whose zealous love of language and unbridled enthusiasm for life inspire their "aged" aunt to continue creating "oulandish" stuff for young readers. May the words in this book tickle your tongues and prick your hearts!　　　　J. M.

To my mother, Mary　　　　K. B.

Chariot Books is an imprint of David C. Cook Publishing Co.

David C. Cook Publishing Co., Elgin, Illinois 60120
David C. Cook Publishing Co., Weston, Ontario

THE BIBLE READ-TO-ME ABC BOOK

© 1988 by Joy MacKenzie for text and Kathleen Bullock for illustrations.

Cover design by Dawn Lauck.

First Printing, 1988
Printed in Singapore

93 92 91 90 89 88 5 4 3 2 1

Library of Congress Cataloging-in-Publication Data
MacKenzie, Joy.
  The Bible read-to-me ABC book / by Joy Mackenzie.
    p. cm.
  Summary: Depicts scenes from Bible stories arranged by the letters of the alphabet, from the Angel who spoke to Mary about the birth of Jesus to the Zany Zoo carried by Noah in his ark.
  ISBN 1-55513-861-6
  1. Bible—Illustrations. 2. Alphabet—Juvenile literature.
  [1. Bible stories. 2. Alphabet.] I. Title.
BS560.M36 1988
220.9 505—dc19
[E]

A AN ANGEL'S ANNOUNCEMENT
Luke 1:26-38

The angel Gabriel tells Mary that she will be the mother of Jesus.

To Mary of Nazareth, A Message of great Importance from the Lord

About 9 mos. B.C.

ANCESTOR ADAM'S ADAM'S APPLE

B BABEL'S BUNGLING BUILDERS BABBLING
Genesis 11:1-8

Silly men try to build a tower to Heaven so that they can become great and famous.

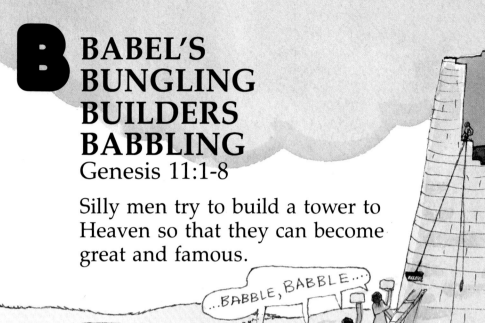

BABYLON'S BELSHAZZAR BEWILDERED
Daniel 5:1-30

A king sees a hand writing a strange message on the palace wall.

BALAAM'S BARNYARD BUDDY BALKING
Numbers 22:21-34

A donkey sees an angel with a sword and stops on the road.

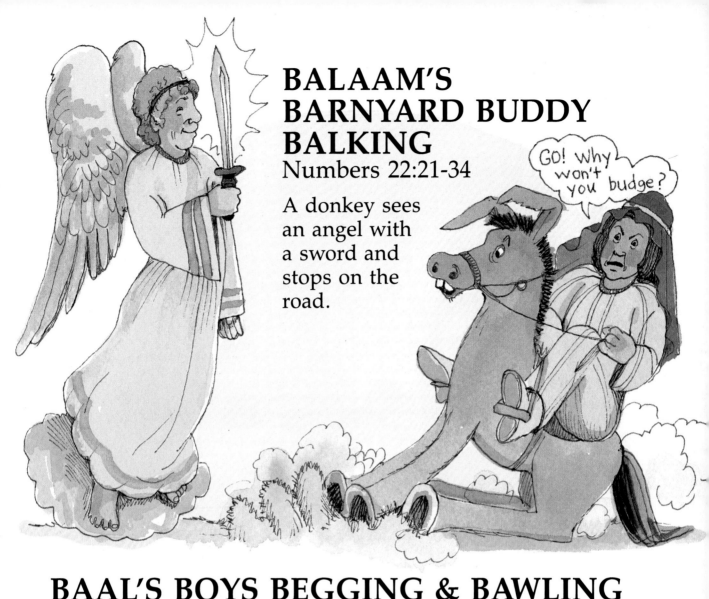

BAAL'S BOYS BEGGING & BAWLING
Worshippers of the false god, Baal, ask him to show them his power, but nothing happens!

I Kings 18:16-39

C

COLORFUL COAT
Genesis 37:2, 3

A father makes a
beautiful coat for his
favorite son.

COMELY COUSIN . . . CHOSEN . . . COURAGEOUS!
Book of Esther

Mordecai's beautiful cousin, Esther, is chosen as King Xerxes's queen and is able to stop a wicked plan against her people.

DEVIOUS DELILAH DEVISING DEVILISH DEED Judges 16:4-21

Samson allows a pretty girl to trick him into telling her the secret of his strength.

ELIJAH'S EXTRAORDINARY EXIT   II Kings 2:1-11

When the time comes for Elijah to go to heaven, he does not die. God comes to get him in a magnificent chariot!

E

EXPEDIENT ESCAPE   Acts 9:22-25

Saul's friends help him with a secret, nighttime escape.

FISH FEELING FAINT & FEVERISH
Jonah 1:1—3:3

FRAIL, FRIGHTENED FUGITIVE

A disobedient prophet is thrown into the sea and swallowed by a great fish—but the story has a happy ending!

GOLIATH'S GALOSHES GA-LUMPHING
I Samuel 17:1-50

Such big feet! But the boy, David, is not afraid of the giant because God is with him.

HAPPY HOMECOMING
Luke 15:11-31

A loving father is
glad to see his
son, who had
run away.

IMPRISONED
Acts 12:3-19

Peter is in prison for being a Christian.

IMMOBILIZED

God causes the guards to fall asleep while He sends an angel to rescue Peter.

JEERING JEZEBEL JANGLING JEWELRY
II Kings 9:20

Evil, selfish Queen Jezebel does not have a happy story.

JEHU'S JAZZY JALOPY

Jehu, a king of Israel, is a wild and crazy driver. He hates the wicked Jezebel.

ALL KINDS OF KINGS
I Timothy 6:15

Jesus, the youngest king of all,
is King of Kings!

LITTLE LOST LAMB . . . LOVED
Matthew 18:12-14

A good shepherd leaves his flock to find one, small lost sheep.

LIVE-AGAIN LAZARUS
John 11:1-44

Lazarus, who was dead, comes alive again when Jesus calls his name.

LENGTHY LEVIATHAN LOUNGING LAZILY Job 41:1-34

God tells His servant, Job, about a strong and fierce sea creature.

M MANNA MONSOON
Exodus 16:11-18, 31, 32

God feeds His people with bread from Heaven. (It was white and tasted like wafers made with honey.)

MIRACLE MEDICINE
Numbers 21:4-9

Disobedient Israelites, bitten by poisonous snakes, are healed by looking at a brass snake on a pole.

METHUSELAH MAKING MERRY

Genesis 5:27

♪♪ HAPPY BIRTHDAY UNCLE METHUSELAH, HAPPY BIRTHDAY TO YOU! ♪

Methuselah is the oldest man who
ever lived. He had 969 birthdays!

NATIVITY
Luke 2:1-20

OVERTURNED
Acts 20:9-19

Eutychus gets sleepy during a long sermon and falls from his seat on the window ledge.

OUCH! Ezra 9:3

Ezra is so upset by the sinful deeds of his people that he tears out his own hair!

PROPHET'S PARADE

Prophets are wise men and women, chosen by God
to take His special messages to people.
Some of their names are fun to say!

ELIJAH

ISAIAH

JEREMIAH

HULDAH

ZECHARIAH

OBADIAH

HABAKKUK

DEBORAH

EZEKIEL

HAGGAI

MALACHI

PECULIAR PATHWAY
Exodus 14:21, 22

Moses stretches his hand over the
sea, and God uses a strong wind
to blow the sea back and make a
path of dry land.

QUAKE Acts 16:16-40

Paul and Silas are in jail for telling people about Jesus.
An earthquake shakes the prison, and some wonderful
things happen!

R REALLY RELIABLE, RELEVANT RULES

The Golden Rule
Luke 6:31

"Do to others as you would have them do to you."

The Great Commandment
Luke 10:27

"Love the Lord your God with all your heart and with all your soul and with all your strength and with all your mind"; and, "Love your neighbor as yourself."

RARE ROD
Genesis 22:13

Aaron's rod becomes a snake and swallows up other snakes!

REMARKABLE RESCUE
Matthew 8:23-27

Jesus stills a wild storm and keeps the fishermen safe.

S

SECRET SAILOR
Exodus 1:22—2:10

The baby Moses is hidden from a wicked
Pharaoh . . . in a floating basket!

SALT STATUE . . . SAD
Genesis 19:24-26

Lot's wife disobeys God's order and turns into a statue of salt!

SARAH'S SURPRISE
Genesis 21:1-7

Sarah thought she was much too old to have a child . . . but God loves surprises!

TREMBLING THOMAS TOUCHES
John 20:25-29

Thomas feels the nail scars in Jesus' hands.

Genesis 27:1-29

TWO TERRIBLE TRICKS

Genesis 29:16-30

Rebekah helps her son Jacob deceive his father.

When Jacob becomes a man, Laban promises that Jacob can marry his daughter Rachel. But instead, he brings his daughter Leah to be Jacob's bride.

U UNFORGETTABLE!!!
Genesis 9:12-17

The rainbow reminds us of God's
promise that He will never
again flood all the earth with water.

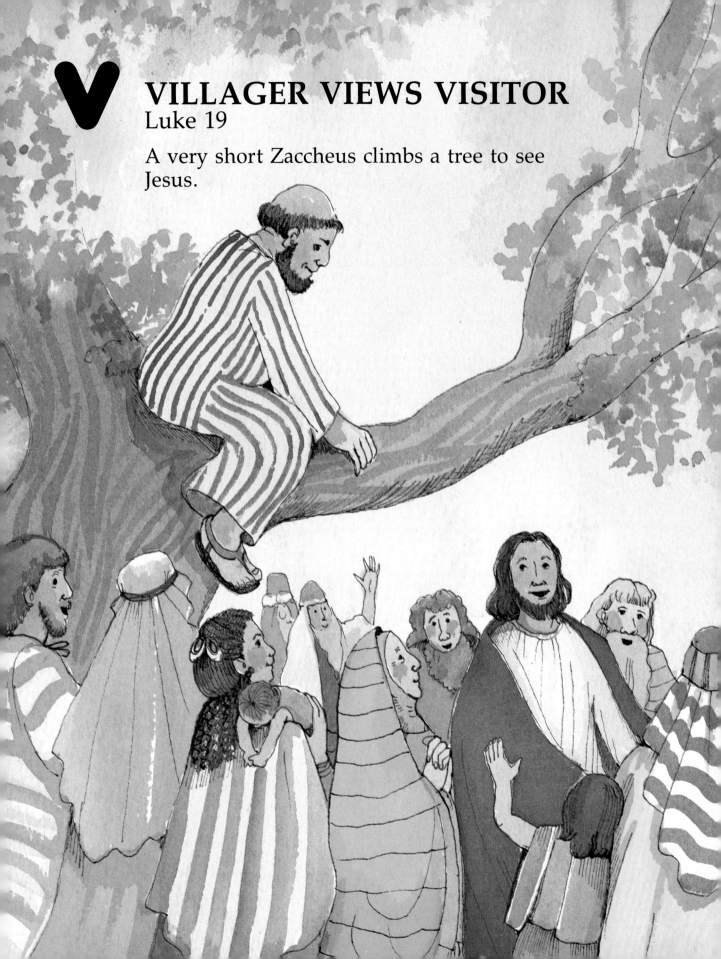

VILLAGER VIEWS VISITOR
Luke 19

A very short Zaccheus climbs a tree to see Jesus.

WONDERFUL WEDDING WINE
John 2:1-11

A bridegroom runs out of wine for his guests at the wedding feast. Jesus performs His first miracle and helps His friend by turning six big jars of water into the best wine the guests have ever tasted!

VERY VERSATILE VEHICLE

GLORY TO GOD IN THE HIGHEST, AND ON EARTH, PEACE,

EXTRA-TERRESTIAL EXCITEMENT
Luke 2:8-14

Lots and lots of angels tell the shepherds about Jesus' birth.

YEA!!!!
Matthew 28:1-8

Jesus is risen from the dead!

ZANY ZOO Genesis 7:13-16

Every kind of living creature sails on the ark with Noah.

_____'s ABC PAGE

Write your name on the line above. Then write your ABC's in the spaces below. Make them perfectly beautiful! Can you find a picture in the book to go with each letter?

Aa Bb Cc Dd Ee Ff Gg Hh Ii
Jj Kk Ll Mm Nn Oo Pp Qq
Rr Ss Tt Uu Vv Ww Xx Yy Zz

Aa